CONTENTS

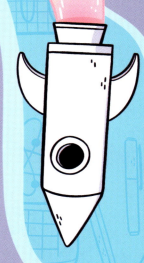

WHAT IS PHYSICS?

Absolutely everything in the Universe, from a giant galaxy of stars to the tiniest grain of sand, is made of matter. You, me and the air we breathe are made of matter, and so is this book.

Physics is the study of matter – what it's made of, how it came to be, the way it behaves and how different types of matter interact with each other.

Physicists try to understand and explain the things that make up our world, such as light, sound, energy, movement and time. Physics also helps other scientists. It allows engineers to design and construct machines and buildings; researchers to develop new medicines and treatments; and earth scientists to predict earthquakes, hurricanes and volcanic eruptions.

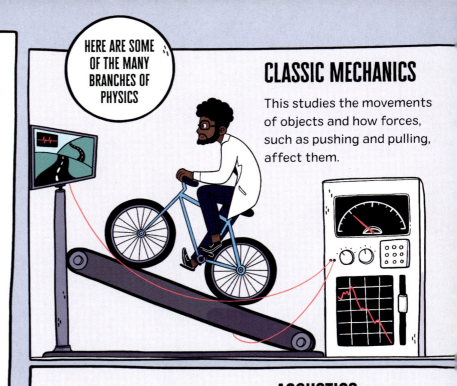

HERE ARE SOME OF THE MANY BRANCHES OF PHYSICS

CLASSIC MECHANICS

This studies the movements of objects and how forces, such as pushing and pulling, affect them.

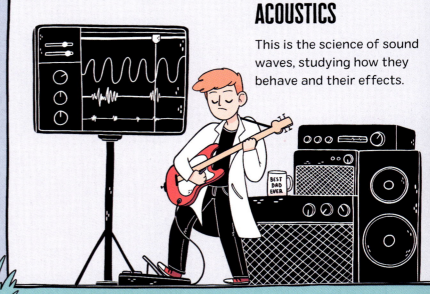

ACOUSTICS

This is the science of sound waves, studying how they behave and their effects.

PHYSICS IN HISTORY

They may not have realised it, but even the earliest humans studied physics – how the Sun and Moon create day and night, the best design for a fishing spear, or how to make fire to cook their freshly caught food.

Ancient Greek astronomers worked out that Earth is round, but wrongly thought that the Sun orbited Earth.

In the **1600s**, experiments by the Italian scientist Galileo proved that different objects fall through the air at the same speed, no matter how heavy they are.

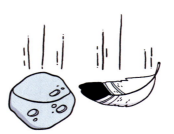

In the late **1660s**, scientist Isaac Newton described gravity as an invisible force that pulls objects towards each other, after he saw an apple fall from a tree.

everyday STEM

SCIENCE

PHYSICS

Science is all around you!

KINGFISHER

First published 2022 by Kingfisher
an imprint of Macmillan Children's Books
The Smithson, 6 Briset Street, London, EC1M 5NR
Associated companies throughout the world
www.panmacmillan.com

Series editor: Lizzie Davey
Series design: Jim Green
Text by Dr Shini Somara and Rona Skene
Illustrations by Luna Valentine

ISBN: 978-0-7534-4676-8

9 8 7 6 5 4 3 2 1
1TR/0322/WKT/UG/128MA

EU representative: 1st Floor, The Liffey Trust Centre,
117-126 Sheriff Street Upper, Dublin 1 D01 YC43

A CIP catalogue record for this book is available from the British Library.

Printed in China

FSC
www.fsc.org
MIX
Paper from
responsible sources
FSC® C116313

OPTICS

Optics investigates light and how it behaves when it meets and interacts with other objects.

ELECTROMAGNETISM

This branch of physics studies how electricity and magnetism combine to form a powerful force, in both nature and technology.

THERMODYNAMICS

Scientists look at the connections between heat and other kinds of energy.

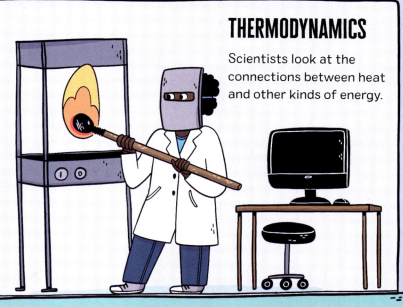

In the **1800s**, English chemist John Dalton proved the existence of atoms – tiny, seemingly indestructible particles that make up all the matter in the Universe.

In the early **20th century**, German-American physicist Albert Einstein helped transform physics with his revolutionary theories about space, time, gravity and the behaviour of atoms.

$$E = mc^2$$

Theories about how our Universe works can be really wacky. The physics research organization, CERN in Switzerland, was founded in **1954**. Here, scientists have built a gigantic track for atoms to whizz round and then hopefully smash into each other. Atom collisions help scientists understand how the Universe began.

MOTION

Everything in the Universe is on the move, even when it looks as if it's completely still. This is because everything has energy that it uses to move or change in some way. Atoms vibrate with energy as the electrons inside them orbit their nucleus. Earth and other planets move around the Sun, and the Sun itself moves within its galaxy. Everything moves at its own speed. Even Earth's surface is moving – just very, very slowly.

FRAMES OF REFERENCE

Physicists use the word "motion" to mean a change in position compared to a fixed point. This point is called the frame of reference, and it can be either a place or an object that stays in its original place. For example, the starting blocks are a frame of reference for an athlete starting a race. We think of the blocks as not moving but of course they are, because all the time Earth is both spinning on its axis and moving round the Sun.

VELOCITY AND SPEED

Speed and velocity are two ways to describe how an object moves. Speed is the time it takes an object to move a set distance. Velocity describes an object's speed in a certain direction. If the car's direction changes, its velocity changes too, even if its speed stays the same.

NEWTON'S LAWS OF MOTION

More than 300 years ago, a brilliant scientist called Isaac Newton came up with a set of rules that explain how an object will behave when a force acts on it. The rules set out what causes the object to move, or stop moving, and what makes it move faster, slow down or go in a different direction. Scientists still apply Newton's laws to almost all objects, although we now know that different laws apply to very small objects such as atoms and light particles.

Newton's First Law is that any object will either stay still, or keep moving at the same speed, unless another force acts on it. So, a football does not move until you apply force by kicking it. It will then carry on moving until another force stops it.

SIR ISAAC NEWTON
(1643–1727)

Isaac Newton was one of the most original thinkers in the history of science. A brilliant student, he became a professor of mathematics when he was only 26 years old. His *Principia Mathematica* ("Principles of Mathematics") is one of the most important science books ever written. As well as coming up with the Laws of Motion and his theory of gravity, he also invented the first-ever reflecting telescope, invented a new type of mathematics called calculus and was one of the first scientists to observe that white light can be split into a spectrum of colour. What an amazing career!

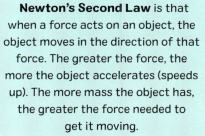

Newton's Second Law is that when a force acts on an object, the object moves in the direction of that force. The greater the force, the more the object accelerates (speeds up). The more mass the object has, the greater the force needed to get it moving.

Newton's Third Law is that whenever two objects meet, they apply equal and opposite forces on each other. Another way of saying this is "every action has an equal and opposite reaction". So when a rocket blasts off, the engine pushes out a downward stream of super-hot gases. The reaction is a huge upward force which thrusts the rocket into the sky.

FORCES

Forces are what drives everything that happens in the Universe, from a grasshopper jumping off a leaf to the International Space Station orbiting Earth. Forces push or pull objects to speed them up, slow them down, send them in another direction or squash or stretch them into a new shape. Forces are invisible, but we see and feel their effects every minute of every day.

The impact of a force on an object can be described by an equation:

"F" is the total (net) force

"a" is the acceleration that occurs

$$F = ma$$

"m" is the object's mass

BALANCED FORCES

When two or more forces act on an object, they can combine to make a greater force. However, if the forces are equal and acting in opposite directions, they cancel each other out and nothing happens. A bridge is a complex structure, with different forces pushing and pulling in different directions. But because the forces are balanced (assuming that the engineer got it right!) the bridge is stable and doesn't move.

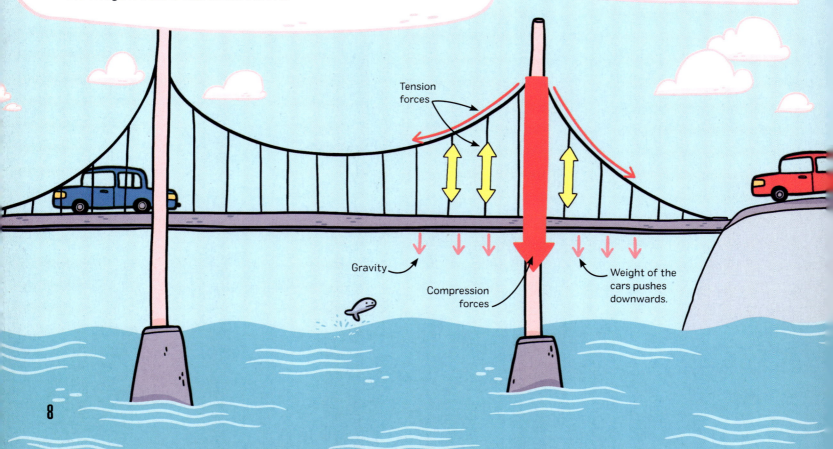

Tension forces

Gravity

Compression forces

Weight of the cars pushes downwards.

TYPES OF FORCE

There are many different types of force. Without them, there would be no life on Earth. Our bodies rely on forces to keep us going: they pump blood round our system, pull air into our lungs, push waste gases out as we exhale and help us to walk, run and even sleep!

Friction slows surfaces down as they rub against other.

Gravity is the force that pulls you towards the ground.

Magnetism pulls certain objects togther or pushes them apart.

Applied force is what you use when you push a trolley.

Buoyancy is an upwards force that keeps objects in the air, such as balloons.

Tension is created by pulling along an object, such as a dog's lead.

Drag slows down something moving through air or water.

Spring force is the result of stretching or squeezing a spring.

DID YOU KNOW?

In deep space there are no forces such as gravity or atmospheric resistance to act against forward motion. If you were to throw a ball here it would just keep on moving in a straight line, at the same speed for ever!

WORK, ENERGY AND HEAT

To most of us, work is the opposite of play: it's homework, doing the washing up or tidying your room. In physics though, work is what happens when a force acts on an object to move it a certain distance. The distance over which the force acts is really important.

WORK

Work is calculated as the force times the distance in the direction of the force.

Work = Force x Distance

1. If you push against something that isn't moveable, no work has occurred – no matter how puffed out you are! No distance travelled means no work has occurred.

2. If you hold a basket up over your head while you walk to a picnic spot, there's no work because the upward force you use to carry the basket is in a different direction to the distance the basket travels.

3. If you use force to do a press-up, lifting your body up and back down – again, there's no work! This is because the total distance travelled from the start of the press-up to the end point back on the ground is zero.

4. If you let go of an object and let it drop to the floor, work does occur. The force of gravity has done work, moving the object from your hand to a different place – the ground.

ENERGY

Energy is what makes everything in the Universe happen. It's the ability to exert a force that will cause an object to move or change.

Energy comes in different forms, which are closely connected. Often, one kind of energy will change into another. For example, using a kettle turns electrical energy into thermal energy (heat).

Energy that is stored to be used later is called potential energy. When it is used to make something move, it transforms into kinetic (moving) energy.

TYPES OF ENERGY

Mechanical

Thermal

Nuclear

Chemical

Electromagnetic

Sonic

Gravitational

Kinetic

Potential

Ionization

HEAT ENERGY

The energy of hot things is called heat energy or thermal energy. When an object's atoms gain more energy, it makes them move around faster. This movement is what creates heat.

If you take an ice cube out of the freezer, it's solid because its atoms are clumped together and moving very slowly. As the ice takes energy from the warmer air, the atoms start moving more and break free of their clumps. The ice becomes water. If you add even more energy, the atoms move much more quickly. Eventually, they break free from each other and escape into the air as steam.

Using heat energy

Steam is full of atoms that are bursting with energy. It can be used to spin a turbine, which transforms the heat energy into electricity.

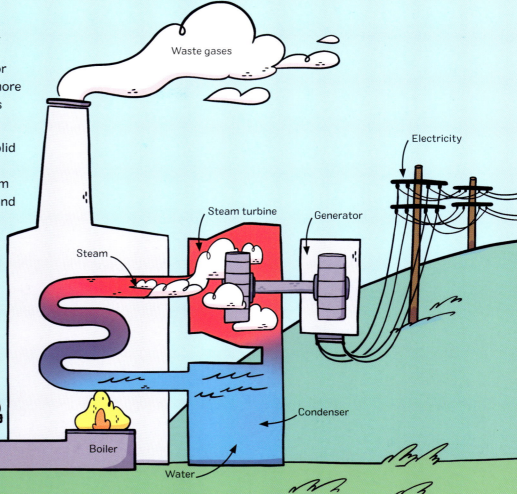

Waste gases

Electricity

Steam turbine

Generator

Steam

Coal

Condenser

Air

Boiler

Water

MARIA GOEPPERT MAYER
(1906-1972)

Maria Goeppert Mayer's work on the structure of an atom's nucleus won her the Nobel Prize for Physics in 1963. She was only the second woman to win this prize, after Marie Curie 60 years earlier. Her "Nuclear Shell Model" theory explained the ways that certain atoms behaved, which had up to then puzzled scientists. Through her research, Goeppert Mayer's also made important discoveries in chemical, atomic and laser physics.

LIGHT AND DARK MATTER

Light is a form of energy that is made inside atoms that have become excited. But exactly how does an atom get into that state? It's all down to how electrons orbit around the atom's nucleus.

Light from the Sun is the major source of energy for every living thing on the planet, including us.

WHAT IS LIGHT?

Light is a type of energy called electromagnetic radiation. When an object heats up, the electrons inside atoms become extra-active. The electrons' excess energy is then released in the form of tiny bundles of energy called photons – these are what we see as light.

HOW DOES LIGHT TRAVEL?

This might seems like a simple question, but actually physicists have been arguing about the answer forever! Mostly, light behaves like a wave, such as when it bounces off a mirror, making an exact reflection. So scientists believed that light travels in waves – until Albert Einstein came along! He showed that light can also act as if it were a stream of tiny particles. Most physicists now believe that light is both a particle and a wave at the same time. Scientists gave this its own name – wave-particle duality.

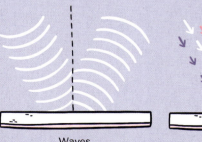

Waves   Particles

VERA RUBIN (1928-2016)

Vera Rubin was an American physicist whose discoveries changed how we think about the Universe. She loved astronomy even as a child, and built her own cardboard telescope when she was a teenager.

Rubin's studies of how stars move within spiral galaxies eventually led her to a mind-boggling conclusion – that these galaxies were held together by something invisble but incredibly heavy, which she called dark matter. She calculated that most of the Universe is made of this mysterious matter, and that its gravity is what helps to keep the Universe together.

DARK MATTER AND DARK ENERGY

Scientists' observations have led them to think that stars, galaxies and planets are all held together by "something". We can't see it because light doesn't bounce off it – but we can see the effect that it has on things around it. This "something" is two things: dark matter, a force of gravity that pulls the Universe together; and dark energy, a force that does the opposite, pushing everything apart and expanding the Universe.

WHAT IS IN THE UNIVERSE?

Matter we can see: 5%

Dark matter 27%

Dark energy 68%

BLACK HOLE

They're not holes, and they're not made of dark matter either! A black hole forms when a giant star collapses under its own weight. It looks like a hole because its gravity is so strong that nothing can escape it, not even light.

ELECTROMAGNETISM

Electricity and magnetism play separate, important roles, but when they join together, they form a real force to be reckoned with – electromagnetism. Electromagnetism is absolutely essential to our world: it powers the interactions between atoms, matter and energy.

WHAT IS ELECTRICITY?

Electricity is a type of energy in the form of charged particles called electrons. These particles can flow through a material to create an electrical current. Electrical current travels along cables and wires above or below ground into our homes. Electrical charges that build up in one place become static electricity. Lightning is caused by static electricity moving between clouds and the ground.

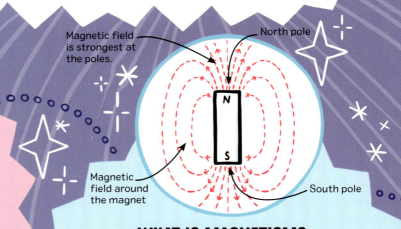

Magnetic field is strongest at the poles.

North pole

Magnetic field around the magnet

South pole

WHAT IS MAGNETISM?

Magnetism is an invisible force that pushes objects together or pulls them apart. This force comes from electrons inside a magnet's atoms. Magnetism works more strongly on some materials, such as iron, than others, such as plastic. A magnet has two ends, called poles. Between them is the magnetic field, the zone into which the objects the magnet attracts will be pulled.

Earth is a giant magnet, because its core is made of magnetic molten iron. It's so powerful that all the world's magnets line up with Earth's magnetic field. This is why a compass will always point north.

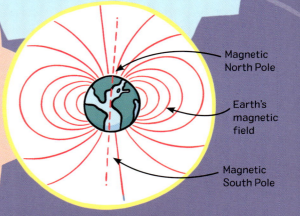

Magnetic North Pole

Earth's magnetic field

Magnetic South Pole

ELECTROMAGNETISM

Electricity and magnetism are closely related – both are created by the actions of electrons inside atoms. An electrical current always creates a magnetic field around it, and if you wrap a current-carrying wire around an iron bar, the bar will become a magnet, too. This is electromagnetism. As soon as the current stops flowing, the bar stops being magnetic.

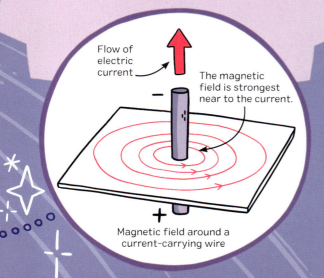

Flow of electric current

The magnetic field is strongest near to the current.

Magnetic field around a current-carrying wire

ELECTROMAGNETS IN USE

A magnet that you can turn on and off easily is incredibly useful. For example, with an electromagnet on a crane, you can pick metal items up, move them, then shut off the current to drop them. Electromagnetism can produce very strong magnets.

MICHAEL FARADAY
(1791–1867)

Michael Faraday is the scientist who put electromagnetism on the map! In 1821, Faraday invented the first ever electric motor, which converted electromagnetic energy into movement. He didn't stop there though: he also invented the transformer, a device to reduce voltage in electrical tools and make them safe to use. Another of his inventions was the dynamo, the first electric generator, which used magnets to convert movement energy into electricity. All three of these inventions still play a key part in a lot of our modern technology and electric gadgets.

EXPERIMENTAL PHYSICS

Experiments are essential in science. If you have an idea or a theory about how the world works, the best way to test it is with an experiment. If you get the answer that you were expecting, that's great. If not... also great! Experiments that go wrong are often as useful as the ones that go well, giving you new ideas for ways to develop your theory. Here are some exceptional experiments that changed the way we understand the world.

1589: GALILEO SHOWS THAT ALL OBJECTS FALL AT THE SAME SPEED

Italian scientist Galileo Galilei climbed a famous tower to show that all falling objects accelerate at the same rate, whatever their size, shape or mass. This gave other scientists their first clue about gravity, the invisible force that pulls objects downwards.

Leaning Tower of Pisa

White light is shone into the prism.

Spectrum emerges, made of the colours red, orange, yellow, green, blue, indigo and violet.

1672: ISAAC NEWTON SPLITS WHITE LIGHT INTO COLORS

Isaac Newton was using a tool called a prism to study light beams when he discovered that the white light came out of the other side of the prism as seven different colours. When he passed the coloured beams through another prism, they combined again to make a single white light. Newton worked out that light was actually made up of a mixture of colours: a discovery that eventually led to today's colour TV screens and computer monitors.

1798: HENRY CAVENDISH WEIGHS THE WORLD

English scientist Cavendish used a clever contraption called a torsion balance to estimate the density of our planet. He used it to observe how gravity moved different-sized lead balls suspended on a wire. Cavendish's careful calculations turned out to be amazingly accurate. He estimated that Earth was 5.48 times denser than water, which was within 1 per cent of the correct value.

1801: THOMAS YOUNG PROVES LIGHT IS A WAVE - OR DOES HE?

In 1801, English physicist Thomas Young performed the simple but fiendishly clever double-slit experiment. He believed that light was made of waves. To prove this, he aimed a beam of light at a screen with two small slits and observed the pattern they made on another screen. The light beams formed ripples, just like waves of water on a pond, overlapping then merging. He was partly right. Today, scientists believe light is a wave, but that it's also made of particles.

1953: ROSALIND FRANKLIN PHOTOGRAPHS DNA

Using a method called X-ray crystalography, Franklin made the first-ever images of DNA, the molecule that carries the chemical "code" to build cells in every living thing. Her discovery that DNA is shaped like a twisted ladder (called a double helix), helped scientists to understand how DNA molecules duplicate themselves to make new cells.

1932: ERNEST RUTHERFORD AND HIS TEAM SPLIT THE ATOM

Rutherford discovered that by bombarding atoms of nitrogen with alpha rays, he could split the atoms apart. This released tiny particles called protons, and turned the nitrogen into oxygen. Rutherford had invented a brand-new science – nuclear physics. Later, scientists worked out how to collect and use the huge energy created by splitting atoms.

1851: HIPPOLYTE FIZEAU MEASURES THE SPEED OF LIGHT

French scientist Fizeau directed light pulses at a spinning, toothed wheel. A few kilometres away, a mirror reflected the light back through the wheel. Fizeau adjusted the wheel's speed until each pulse that went through a gap one way was blocked by the next tooth on its return. By measuring the speed of the wheel and the distance to the mirror, Fizou could work out how fast the light was traveling, and his answer – 315,000 km/s, was impressively accurate!

1840: JAMES PRESCOTT JOULE DEMONSTRATES THE CONSERVATION OF ENERGY

Joule had a talent for thinking up practical experiments. In one, he discovered that when he used a simple machine to turn a paddle wheel in water, the water got hotter. He worked out that the mechanical energy had been transformed into heat energy. From this, he realised that the energy in the Universe is never lost or used up – it just transforms into a different kind of energy.

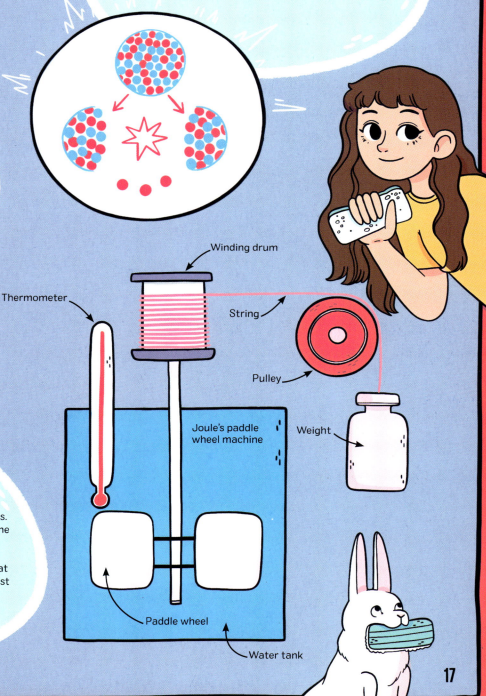

Winding drum

Thermometer

String

Pulley

Joule's paddle wheel machine

Weight

Paddle wheel

Water tank

THEORETICAL PHYSICS

Theoretical physicists tend not to do experiments themselves. Instead, they look at the data from experiments and try to explain the results, or predict what might happen in future experiments. They use their imagination to work out what the data means. They might also suggest further experiments to collect data that might help to prove or disprove their ideas and theories.

GENERAL RELATIVITY

Albert Einstein was one of the greatest theoretical physicists, and his theory of general relativity is one of physics' most important ideas. Einstein saw gravity not as a pulling force, but as being like a sheet of rubber in space. A huge mass like Earth makes a "dent" in the sheet, and the Moon is pulled into Earth's orbit by the "slope" the dent creates. This warping also affects light and even slows down time. Einstein predicted, correctly, that a clock will tick faster in space than on Earth.

QUANTUM COMPUTING

Werner Heisenberg, Nils Bohr and Erwin Schrödinger were 20th-century theoretical physicists who wanted to understand and explain the behaviour of electrons and other tiny particles that move around inside atoms. Their work became a new branch of physics, called quantum mechanics. This knowledge forms the basis of quantum computing. Quantum computers are so complex, that physicists are still working out how to build them. One day they will be so powerful and fast, that the computers we use today will look really slow in comparison.

SHOHINI GHOSE

When Shohini Ghose was a young girl growing up in India, she wanted to be an astronaut. "The first Indian astronaut went to space when I was a child," she said. "I was immediately inspired."

Rakesh Sharma

Ghose watched the US space drama *Star Trek* on TV with her brother every Sunday morning.

Combining her enthusiasm for everything to do with space with her talent for maths and physics, Ghose set her sights on studying the laws that govern the Universe.

Today she is an award-winning quantum physicist and professor of physics and computer science. Ghose has also written a bestselling astronomy textbook.

PHYSICS IN A PLANE

So just how does a huge plane weighing many tonnes get off the ground and stay in the air? Let's discover the amazing physics behind powered flight.

FOUR FORCES

Planes can fly because they create forces to keep them airborne and manage the ones that keep them grounded. The four main forces involved are drag, thrust, weight and lift. Drag pulls a plane backwards, whereas thrust propels it forwards. Weight and lift are also opposites: weight pulls the plane downwards, while lift pushes it up. To fly, a plane has to generate enough thrust and lift to counteract weight and drag.

Air goes in.   Compressor   Turbine

Combustion chamber   Air is pushed out, extremely fast.

THRUST

The jet engines attached to the wings of the plane contain spinning turbines, which suck air in from the front. The air is heated by burning fuel, then blasted out of the back of the engine. As the powerful jet of hot gases shoots backwards, the aeroplane is pushed with just as much power in the opposite direction, forwards. This propulsion, or forward movement, is called thrust.

DRAG

GRAVITY

LIFT

THRUST

LIFT

You might think that engines are key to making a plane fly, but actually lots of things fly without engines, such as kites, gliders or birds. They use lift. In a plane, lift is created by air flowing around the plane's curved wings. The air under the wings moves more slowly and so exerts more pressure than the faster-moving air above the wing. This creates the upward force we call lift.

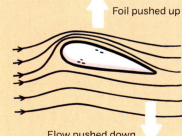

Foil pushed up

Flow pushed down

PHYSICS IN A CAR

As well as using mechanics to make a car move fast and efficiently, physics plays a key part in designing cars that are safer for us to travel in.

SEAT BELT

Newton's Law tells us that an object that's not moving tries to stay that way – this is called inertia. This means that in a collision your seat belt stays in the same place, holding you still while the force of impact tries to thrust you forwards.

CRUMPLE ZONE

Crumple zones at the front and back of the car work by absorbing most of the energy of the impact of a collision before it reaches the passengers.

BRAKE PADS

A car in motion has kinetic energy. Brake pads, when applied to fast-spinning wheels, create a friction force that grips the wheels and slows them down. The friction converts some of the kinetic energy into heat – used brake pads can get very hot!

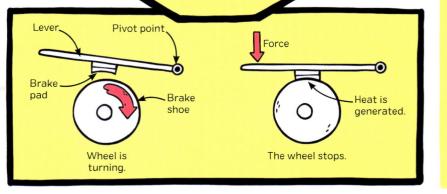

Lever
Pivot point
Brake pad
Brake shoe
Wheel is turning.

Force
Heat is generated.
The wheel stops.

WHAT IS MOMENTUM?

These features are all about slowing down a fast-moving car safely. We call an object's movement momentum. When two cars collide, their total momentum is the same after impact as before. The momentum of each car might change, but the total is the same. We measure momentum by using this calculation:

Momentum = Mass x Velocity

THE WORLD OF WAVES

Electromagnetic waves are really useful – they make the world visible, let us communicate long-distance, cook food and even cure diseases! The electromagnetic spectrum is the name for the whole range of electromagnetic radiation, from the longest to the shortest waves.

THE ELECTROMAGNETIC SPECTRUM

The spectrum includes a range of different types of waves, which we put in categories according to length. All the waves travel at the speed of light and carry streams of particles called photons. The amount of energy in these photons varies. Radio-wave photons have the least energy and the longest waves. At the other end of the spectrum, gamma rays have the shortest waves and their protons are seriously energetic!

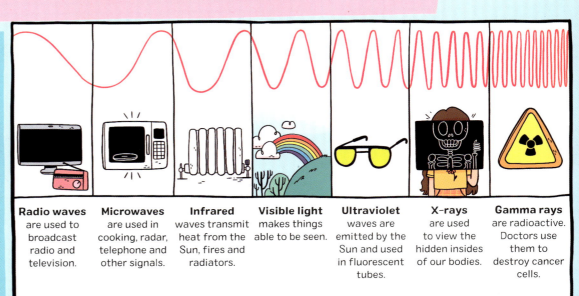

Radio waves are used to broadcast radio and television.

Microwaves are used in cooking, radar, telephone and other signals.

Infrared waves transmit heat from the Sun, fires and radiators.

Visible light makes things able to be seen.

Ultraviolet waves are emitted by the Sun and used in fluorescent tubes.

X-rays are used to view the hidden insides of our bodies.

Gamma rays are radioactive. Doctors use them to destroy cancer cells.

TELEVISION

Radio waves carry signals for radios (obviously!), mobile phones, satnavs and televisions. A TV transmitter turns pictures and sound into a digital code. It sends the code out via radio waves, which are picked up by a reciever, such as an antenna or your TV aerial. The signal then travels by cable into your TV, where it is decoded and turned back into sound and pictures.

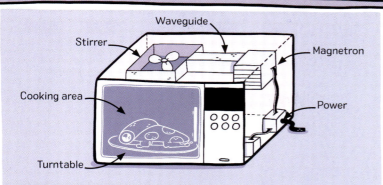

MICROWAVE OVEN

In a microwave oven, the food is bombarded by microwaves – radio waves with a short wavelength – generated by an electron tube called a magnetron. The waves, directed by the waveguide, make water and fat molecules in the food vibrate. The more they vibrate, the hotter they get. Ping! Dinner is served...

HEDY LAMARR (1914–2000)

This Hollywood movie star had a secret – she was also a brilliant inventor. During World War II, Lamarr and her friend George Antheil came up with a way to protect the US Navy's radio-controlled torpedos from being intercepted and diverted by the enemy. They developed a device that could send radio signals in a way Lamarr called "frequency hopping". After the war, her invention was picked up by scientists who developed it into the digital technology behind the mobile phone, bluetooth and wi-fi devices we all rely on today.

REMOTE CONTROL

Infrared waves come after microwaves in the electromagnetic spectrum. When you channel-hop on your TV, the remote control sends out beams of infrared waves that carry digital instructions to the TV. Infrared waves also carry heat – you can "see" the waves if you wear special heat-detecting goggles.

FIBRE OPTICS

Information can travel along waves in many different ways, including as electircal signals along wires and cables or wirelessly via radio waves. Optical fibre works by coding information in a beam of light and sending the beam through a thin glass or plastic pipe, called a fibre-optic cable. The advantage of this is that it's super-quick – light travels faster than anything else we know of. Our TV, internet and telephone networks all rely on fibre-optic technology.

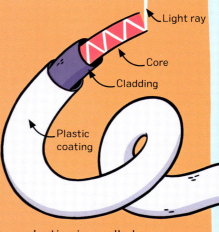

GEOPHYSICS

Geophysicists use their knowledge of physics to study and analyse the structure of planet Earth and what's going on beneath our feet. One important branch of geophysics is seismology, which studies the vibrations caused by earthquakes.

SEISMIC WAVES

All waves are vibrations that transfer energy from one place to another. They can be electromagnetic, like light waves, or mechanical, like sound or ocean waves. Seismic waves – the waves that travel through Earth – are mechanical waves. Seismic waves are at their most powerful at the centre of an earthquake. They can be measured hundreds of kilometres away by a instrument called a seismometer.

WHAT ON EARTH IS EARTH MADE OF?

Right at the centre of the planet is a core of solid iron. Surrounding this is the outer core of molten (semi-melted) metal. Then the thickest layer, the mantle, is made of hot, semi-melted rock. Finally, floating on top of the mantle is Earth's crust, its outside layer, which makes up only around 1 per cent of the whole planet.

EARTHQUAKES

Earth's crust is made up of slow-moving sections of rock called tectonic plates. These plates usually slide harmlessly past each other, but sometimes the edges, called fault lines, can get stuck together. As the stuck plates try to move, pressure builds up until the plates suddenly shift, releasing the stored energy as shockwaves that are felt on Earth's surface as an earthquake.

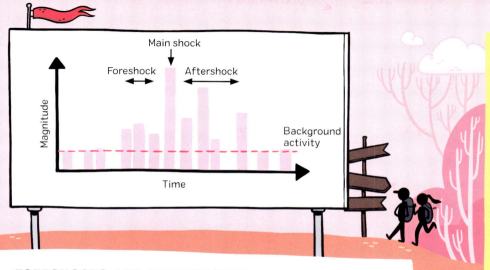

FORESHOCKS AND AFTERSHOCKS

Before an earthquake occurs, there may be smaller tremors called foreshocks. These happen when rocks around the fault line start to move and fracture as the earthquake begins. After the quake there may be tremors, called aftershocks, as the rocks around the fault line settle into new positions. Scientists can't usually identify foreshocks or aftershocks until the whole event is over. Only then can they compare all the shocks and pinpoint the largest one as the main earthquake.

EARTHQUAKE FACTS

The place underground where the earthquake starts is called the hypocentre, or focus. On the surface of Earth, directly above the hypocentre, is the epicentre, where the force of the earthquake will be felt most strongly. Earthquakes are sudden and very hard to predict. The best that geophysicists can do is locate and closely monitor fault lines, as earthquakes are most likely to happen along these cracks in Earth's tectonic plates.

MEASURING EARTHQUAKES

Scientists use seismographs to record the magnitude (size) of seismic waves. The greater the magnitude of the waves, the more powerful (and damaging) an earthquake will be. The Moment Magnitude Scale (MMS) is used to calculate the size of earthquakes. The larger the number on the scale, the more powerful the earthquake.

THE MMS SCALE

< 3: Barely noticeable: you could easily sleep through the action!

4.0: Noticeable but faint vibrations, such as you get when a heavy vehicle passes in front of your house.

6.0: Stronger tremors that everyone will feel. They may cause damage, such as cracks in buildings and broken windows.

7.0: Tremors are strong enough to damage roads and bridges. Some buildings may collapse.

8.0: Collapse of buildings, roads or bridges. Large cracks in the ground may appear.

9.0 and up: Widespread destruction; may flatten whole towns and regions.

OPTICS

Optics is the science of light: what it's made of and how it travels or interacts with different kinds of matter. All physics is useful but optics is super-essential to our daily lives. It has given us lots of really helpful – and fun – inventions: microscopes to study minute bacteria; telescopes to explore the Universe; glasses and contact lenses to help us see better; and cameras and projectors to take and show photos, film and video. Optics is also vital in digital technologies such as microchips, scanners, printers and data transmission.

REFRACTION IN ACTION

Light travels in a straight line until it meets a different medium. So when light travelling through air suddenly hits another substance such as water or glass, the light waves are slowed down. The change in speed makes the light waves change direction slightly, so that we see a distorted image. This bending effect is called refraction.

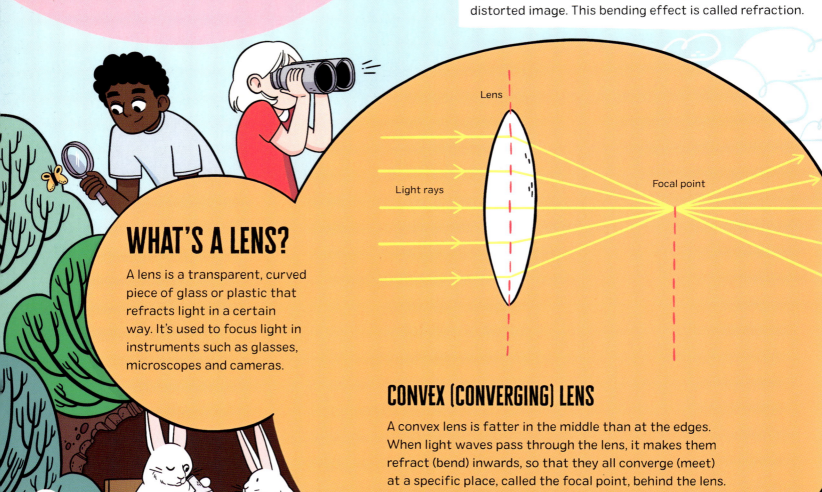

WHAT'S A LENS?

A lens is a transparent, curved piece of glass or plastic that refracts light in a certain way. It's used to focus light in instruments such as glasses, microscopes and cameras.

Lens

Light rays

Focal point

CONVEX (CONVERGING) LENS

A convex lens is fatter in the middle than at the edges. When light waves pass through the lens, it makes them refract (bend) inwards, so that they all converge (meet) at a specific place, called the focal point, behind the lens.

USING LENSES

A convex lens makes objects look nearer and bigger than they are, whereas a concave lens makes things look smaller and farther away. We can uses lenses to perform different tasks, such as in glasses for correcting short-sightedness and spreading out the light beam in a torch.

Microscope

Glasses

Binoculars

Telescope

Torch

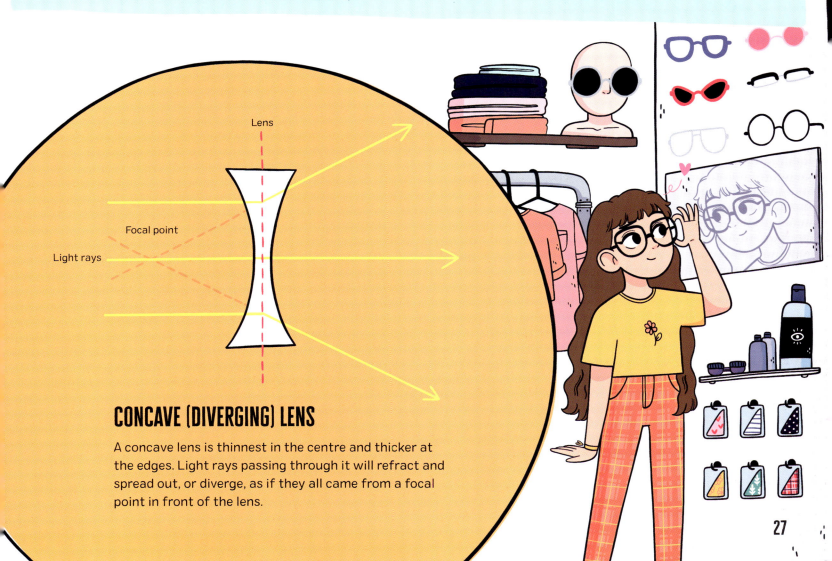

Lens

Focal point

Light rays

CONCAVE (DIVERGING) LENS

A concave lens is thinnest in the centre and thicker at the edges. Light rays passing through it will refract and spread out, or diverge, as if they all came from a focal point in front of the lens.

FAIRGROUND PHYSICS

Forces are very useful, but that doesn't mean they can't be fun, too! At a fairground, many different forces are balanced to produce rides that are super-exciting, but safe to use, so we can enjoy lots of thrills without any spills!

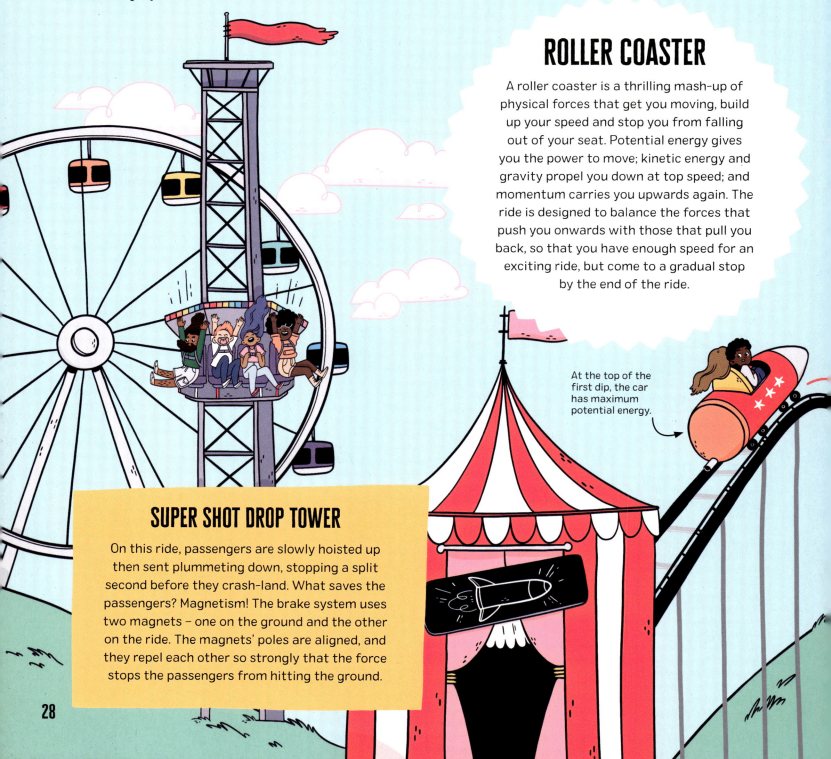

ROLLER COASTER

A roller coaster is a thrilling mash-up of physical forces that get you moving, build up your speed and stop you from falling out of your seat. Potential energy gives you the power to move; kinetic energy and gravity propel you down at top speed; and momentum carries you upwards again. The ride is designed to balance the forces that push you onwards with those that pull you back, so that you have enough speed for an exciting ride, but come to a gradual stop by the end of the ride.

At the top of the first dip, the car has maximum potential energy.

SUPER SHOT DROP TOWER

On this ride, passengers are slowly hoisted up then sent plummeting down, stopping a split second before they crash-land. What saves the passengers? Magnetism! The brake system uses two magnets – one on the ground and the other on the ride. The magnets' poles are aligned, and they repel each other so strongly that the force stops the passengers from hitting the ground.

MEGASPIN

This ride is a bit like being in a washing machine! As the wheel spins faster, you feel as if you are being pinned back to the walls. The wheel is spinning in a circle, driven by centripetal force, which pulls towards the circle's centre. The force making people stick to the walls is a centrifugal force. Your body is trying to travel in a straight line – remember Newton's First Law? – so it pulls equally hard in the opposite direction, pushing you back against the wall.

THE PENDULUM

The Pendulum sways people back and forth on a giant swing. At the top of each swing, you feel weightless, like an astronaut in space. It's not a lack of gravity that causes this – gravity is still there, waiting to pull you down again. It's because, at the top of the swing's arc, your body momentarily loses contact with the seat. This means that the seat is no longer pushing upwards on you, so for that split second you feel as if you are weightless.

The car has enough momentum to reach the second, lower peak.

Momentum from the downward journey allows the car to travel uphill.

Inertia keeps the passengers in their seats, even though gravity is pulling them downwards.

Air resistance and gravity eventually cause the car to lose so much energy that it stops.

HOW DOES A FRIDGE WORK?

How would we manage without fridges? Keeping food cool slows the growth of bacteria that cause food to go off and make us ill. Before fridges, people couldn't do a big shop for fresh food as we do today, as they couldn't store it safely. A fridge works by taking the heat from food inside and moving the heat outside, with the help of a special cooling substance and the natural processes of evaporation and condensation.

5. EVAPORATOR

In the evaporator, the heating and cooling routine starts all over again. As the coolant expands and gets colder, it turns from a liquid into a gas through evaporation. This process cools the air around it. The colder air sinks to the bottom of the fridge, pushing the warmer air upwards towards the cooling coils.

4. EXPANSION VALVE

The cooling liquid now goes through the expansion valve. This lowers the pressure on the coolant, making it even colder before it flows back inside the fridge, to the evaporator.

1. COOLANT

The coolant (or refrigerant) is a substance that changes easily from liquid to gas as it gets hotter or cooler. It travels via metal pipes. As it passes around the fridge, the cold gas absorbs heat from the food. As the gas starts to get hotter, it becomes a liquid and flows downwards to the compressor.

THERMOSTAT

The thermostat controls the temperature of the fridge. When the temperature drops under a certain level, sensors in the thermostat trigger a signal to switch off the compressor. When the temperature rises beyond a set level, it turns the compressor back on.

2. COMPRESSOR

Inside the compressor, the coolant liquid is squeezed and compressed. The pressure makes it heat up until it turns into a gas. This process is called evaporation. The hot gas flows to the condensor.

3. CONDENSER

If you look at the back of a fridge, you will see the condenser, which sits outside the fridge. As the hot coolant passes through the pipes of the condenser, it cools down and turns from a gas back into a liquid in a process called condensation. The heat from the coolant is transferred to the surrounding air by metal fins.

MAGNETS

Magnets are everywhere in your home – can you spot any? Do you have a compass? That needle pointing north is a magnet. The dark strip on a library or membership card is a magnet too, and stores data about you. Home gadgets that have motors, such as food processors or vacuum cleaners, have magnets that switch on when electrical currents flows. Cabinets can have magnetic latches. Even a cat can be a magnet user! Magnetic cat flaps only open for cats wearing magnetic collars.

HOW A MAGNET WORKS

Every magnet has two poles. When the opposite poles of two magnets are close to each other, they are strongly attracted and try to link up. If the same poles are lined up, they will try to get away, or repel, from each other.

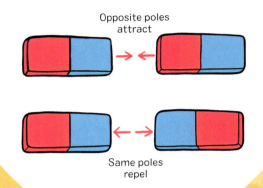

Opposite poles attract

Same poles repel

MAGNETS AND SOUND

The sound that comes out of speakers is based on the interaction between two kinds of magnet – a permanent magnet and an electromagnet.

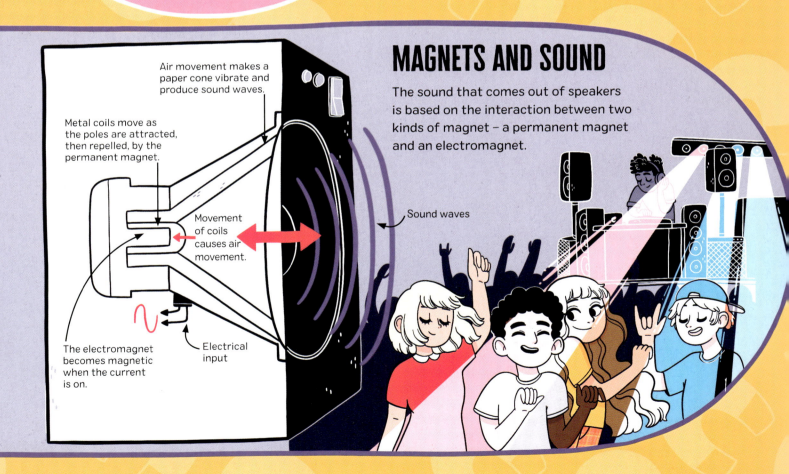

Air movement makes a paper cone vibrate and produce sound waves.

Metal coils move as the poles are attracted, then repelled, by the permanent magnet.

Movement of coils causes air movement.

The electromagnet becomes magnetic when the current is on.

Electrical input

Sound waves

MAGNETS AT WORK

Electrically powered magnets are seriously strong and can be used by cranes to move heavy things like cars and huge iron girders. Magnets also come in handy when you need to separate metal from other materials, such as on a conveyor belt at a recycling centre.

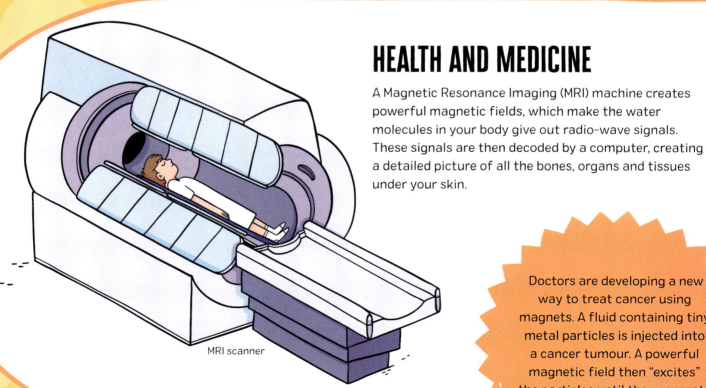

MRI scanner

HEALTH AND MEDICINE

A Magnetic Resonance Imaging (MRI) machine creates powerful magnetic fields, which make the water molecules in your body give out radio-wave signals. These signals are then decoded by a computer, creating a detailed picture of all the bones, organs and tissues under your skin.

Doctors are developing a new way to treat cancer using magnets. A fluid containing tiny metal particles is injected into a cancer tumour. A powerful magnetic field then "excites" the particles until they generate enough heat to kill the cancer cells.

SOUND

Sound is a form of energy made by vibration, which is when something shakes backwards and forwards really fast, like a plucked guitar string. These vibrations travel in invisible waves through air, water or other substances such as wood, rock or metal. The more energy a vibration has, the larger the wave it produces and the louder the noise it makes. As they travel, sound waves gradually spread out and lose energy, so they sound quieter.

SOUND WAVES

Like light, sound travels in waves. But unlike light waves, sound waves must have matter to travel through and cause them to vibrate – even if it's just the atoms that make up air. In a vacuum, where there are no atoms, there's no sound. That's why there are no rock bands in space!

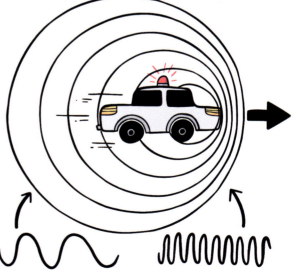

THE DOPPLER SHIFT

Have you noticed how, as an ambulance whizzes past you, its siren's sound seems to change? This is because of something called the Doppler Shift. The siren's sound is sent out in waves at set intervals. As the ambulance gets closer, the gaps between waves (called the frequency) get shorter, making the sound sound higher. After it passes, the gaps become longer and longer as the ambulance gets further away. The frequency is now lower so the siren sounds lower, too.

Still source of sound

Moving source of sound

USING SOUND

Sound is vibrating energy. The power of these vibrations has uses beyond letting us listen to music or chat to friends. Here are two of the surprising ways sound waves make life better for us.

TAKING TEMPERATURE

An acoustic thermometer works by measuring how long it takes for sound to travel along a specially designed gas-filled tube. The warmer the air, the faster the sound travels, because warmer air has more energy. By measuring the time taken by the sound waves, scientists can calculate the temperature around the tube. This thermometer is useful when "normal" thermometers won't work, such as inside a nuclear reactor.

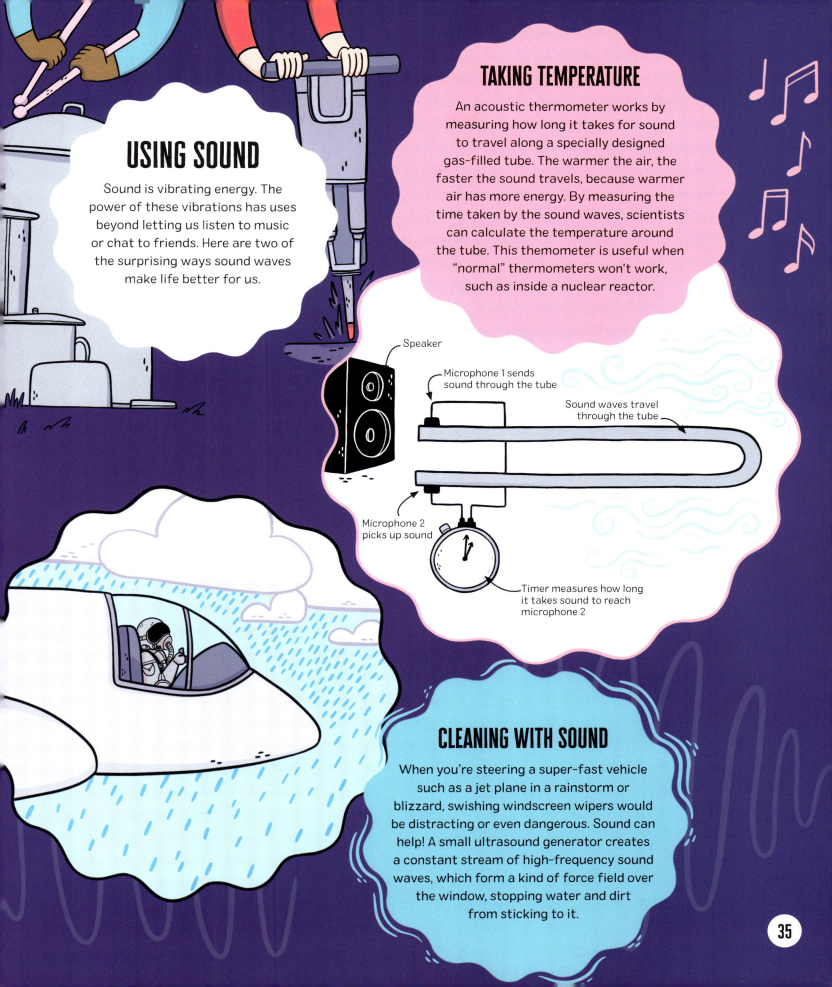

Speaker

Microphone 1 sends sound through the tube

Sound waves travel through the tube

Microphone 2 picks up sound

Timer measures how long it takes sound to reach microphone 2

CLEANING WITH SOUND

When you're steering a super-fast vehicle such as a jet plane in a rainstorm or blizzard, swishing windscreen wipers would be distracting or even dangerous. Sound can help! A small ultrasound generator creates a constant stream of high-frequency sound waves, which form a kind of force field over the window, stopping water and dirt from sticking to it.

THE VERY SMALL

Absolutely everything is made of atoms, and atoms are made of particles. Studying these super-tiny things teaches us about how the Universe works, and how it came to be.

FUNDAMENTAL FORCES

Four basic forces drive the Universe. The first two are gravity and electromagnetism. The other two, called the weak interaction and the strong interaction, hold together the particles inside an atom's nucleus.

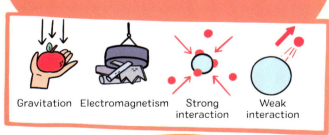

Gravitation   Electromagnetism   Strong interaction   Weak interaction

A UNIVERSE IS BORN

Particle physics might help us understand how the Universe began and expanded. By putting sub-atomic particles in a small space and smashing them together, scientists are trying to recreate the chaotic, high-energy conditions that were present in the moments before and after the Universe was created.

THE STANDARD MODEL

The Standard Model is a theory that tries to explain how the fundamental forces work together. It's a complex idea, explaining that electromagnetic, weak and strong forces result from the action of a special group of force-carrier particles called bosons. But when it comes to gravity, the most familiar force in our world, the Standard Model doesn't work – yet. Physicists today are still working on it. The best explanation for gravity is still the theory of general relativity, which Einstein thought of more than a century ago.

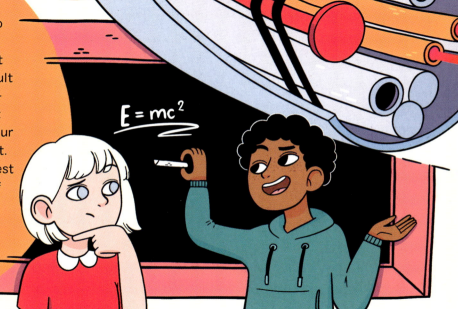

$$E = mc^2$$

SMASH TO LEARN

If you want to find out what's inside anything, from an egg to a personal computer, you first have to break it open. In the same way, physicists smash particles together to split them open so they can see what's going on inside. In order to break up when they collide, the particles have to be travelling at extremely high speeds – almost as fast as the speed of light. To achieve this, physicists have developed huge, high-energy machines called particle accelerators. Particles whizz faster and faster around the accelerator's circuits to reach the correct speed. When they collide, they release the incredibly small, hard-to-find particles that the scientists want to study.

The CERN track is a huge circle, with a circumference of 26.7km.

The biggest particle accelerator in the world is the Large Hadron Collider at CERN, in Europe.

When particles collide, they release even smaller particles called quarks and bosons.

Powerful magnets steer and direct the beams together so that they collide.

Two beams of atomic particles travel round in oppsite directions.

Particle accelerator

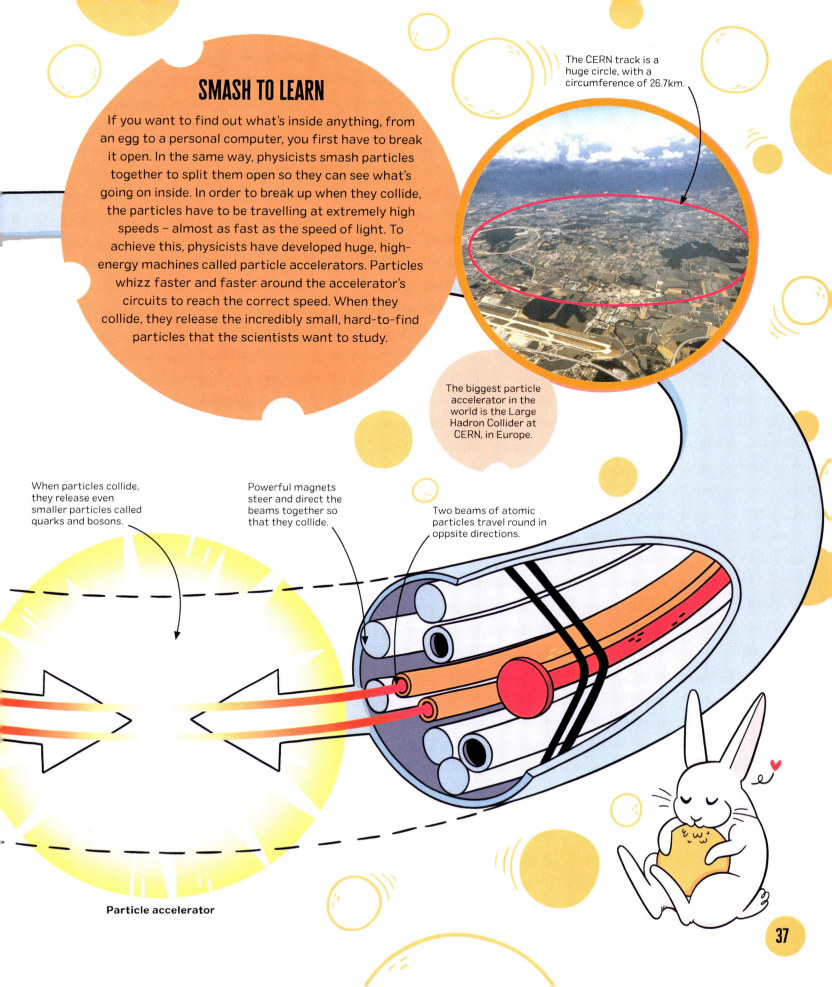

THE VERY BIG

The two branches of physics that look beyond our planet at the stars, planets and phenomena of space are astrophysics and cosmology. Astrophysicists try to understand how the Universe works, and cosmologists study how the Universe came to be and its development over time.

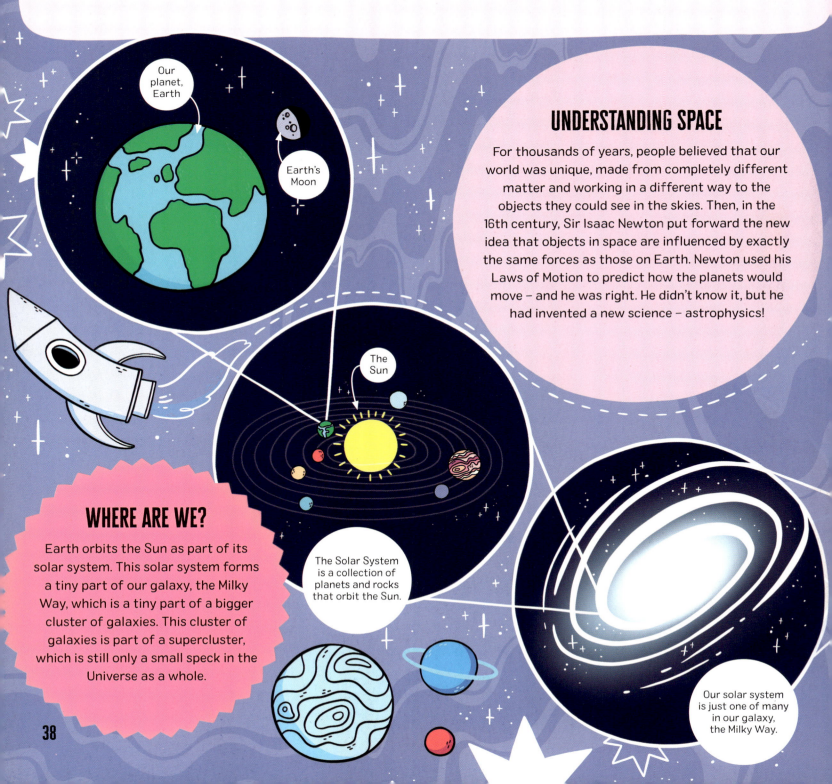

Our planet, Earth

Earth's Moon

UNDERSTANDING SPACE

For thousands of years, people believed that our world was unique, made from completely different matter and working in a different way to the objects they could see in the skies. Then, in the 16th century, Sir Isaac Newton put forward the new idea that objects in space are influenced by exactly the same forces as those on Earth. Newton used his Laws of Motion to predict how the planets would move – and he was right. He didn't know it, but he had invented a new science – astrophysics!

The Sun

WHERE ARE WE?

Earth orbits the Sun as part of its solar system. This solar system forms a tiny part of our galaxy, the Milky Way, which is a tiny part of a bigger cluster of galaxies. This cluster of galaxies is part of a supercluster, which is still only a small speck in the Universe as a whole.

The Solar System is a collection of planets and rocks that orbit the Sun.

Our solar system is just one of many in our galaxy, the Milky Way.

EXPLORING SPACE

Scientists form ideas from what they observe, which makes the telescope an astrophysicist's best friend. In 1990, scientists launched the first telescope into space. Orbiting above Earth's hazy atmosphere, the Hubble Telescope gave us the clearest view yet of the Universe. Missions to probe our solar system and beyond provide space physicists with new information about the planets, stars and matter that make up the Universe.

In 2021, the drone Ingenuity became the first vehicle ever to take off and fly on another planet – Mars.

The observable Universe contains structures called filaments that are made up of superclusters. Between them are vast amounts of empty space.

The James Webb telescope was launched into space on 25 December 2021. It will operate from much further out in space than Hubble does.

The Virgo Supercluster is a collection of around 100 groups of galaxies, including the Local Group.

The Local Group is a group of around 50 galaxies, held together by gravity.

AURORAS

Sometimes you don't even need a telescope to observe amazing space phenomena! The Northern and Southern Lights (aurora borealis and aurora australis) put on a spectacular light show in Earth's polar regions. They occur when streams of charged particles from the Sun hit Earth's magnetic field. The particles then release energy, making gases in the atmosphere glow.

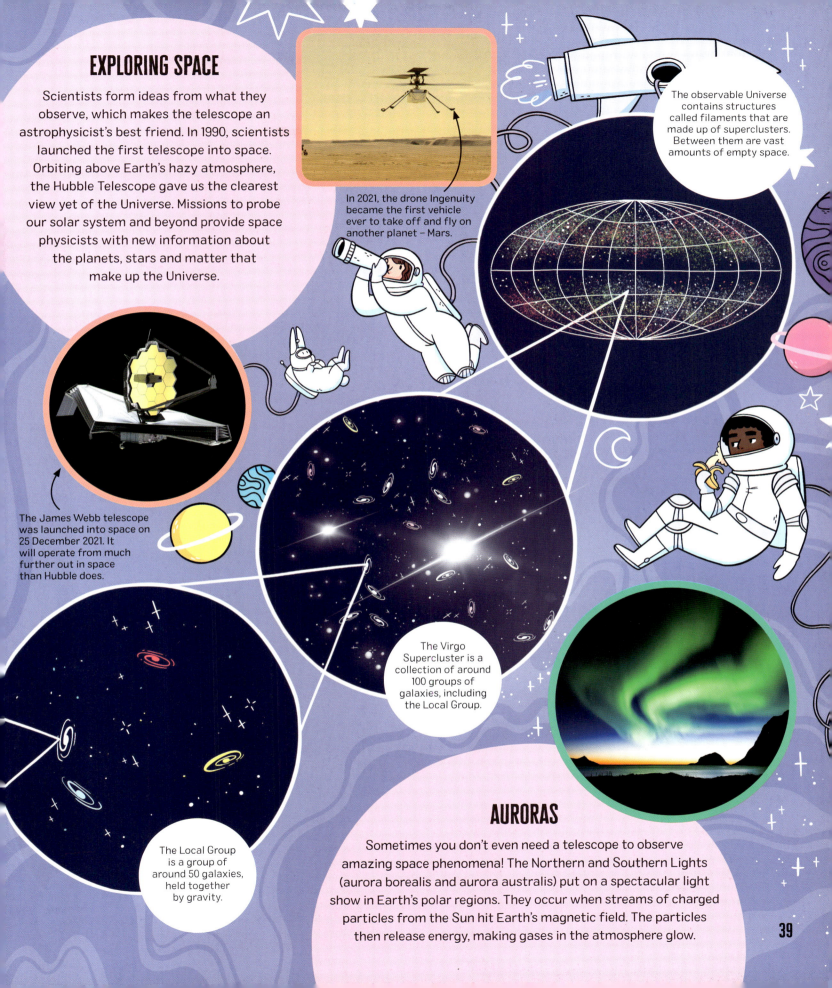

ROBOTICS

Robots are useful because they can do jobs that humans would find too difficult, too dangerous or just too boring!

BUILDING CARS

PICKING FRUIT

EARTHQUAKE RESCUE

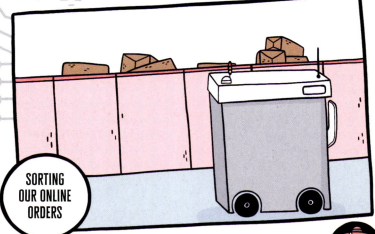

SORTING OUR ONLINE ORDERS

WORKING IN TOXIC ENVIRONMENTS

SMART FABRIC

Scientists in the US have developed a robotic fabric that can change shape, going from soft and cosy to rock-hard in seconds. It looks just like normal cloth, but inside the material is a network of heat sensors and special threads. When the temperature changes, these threads can stiffen, bend and twist themselves into different shapes. The fabric has been used to make a tent that puts itself up, smart clothing and shape-changing machinery.

WHALE NOISE

The North Atlantic right whale is one of the world's most endangered animals. Among the dangers it faces are being hit by passing ships and becoming tangled up in huge fishing nets. To help these whales, scientists have developed technology that listens underwater and teaches itself how the whales communicate with each other. Called machine learning, this means that it's now much easier for ships to detect these animals deep under water. Ships then have plenty of time to change course and leave the whales in peace.

HOW IT WORKS

It's noisier than you think under the sea! As well as the calls of right whales, the listening device picks up lots of other sounds, such as fishing-boat machinery and underwater drilling. A smart device called PAM (passive acoustic monitoring) learns to tell the difference between the noises. It then blocks out the non-whale sounds, so that the animals' calls are clearer and easier to locate.

Research ship

Buoy, with PAM

Whale sound

Whale

VORTEX IN A BOTTLE

A spiral of twisting air or water is called a vortex – you see one every time the water drains out of your bath. In nature, when streams of water or air pull in opposite directions, they create whirlpools and tornados. Here's how to make your very own vortex at home.

YOUR TURN!

YOU WILL NEED
- Two identical, large, clear-plastic bottles
- Water
- Food colouring and glitter
- A washer the same size as the bottle top (you can make one out of card)
- Roll of duct tape

INSTRUCTIONS

1. Fill one of the bottles about three-quarters full of water.

2. Add a little food colouring and glitter – this will make the vortex easier to see.

3. Put the washer on top of the first bottle. Place the mouth of the empty bottle on top of the washer. Use tape to stick the two bottles together tightly.

4. Turn the bottles upside down so that the full one is now on top. Swirl them quickly, to get the water spinning.

5. That's it! Now watch your vortex form.

See how big you can make the vortex by spinning the water faster.

4

5

3

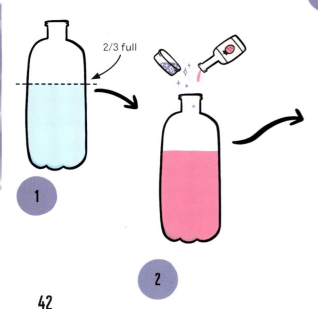

2/3 full

1

2

Use plenty of tape, so the water won't escape.

WHAT'S GOING ON?

The fast-spinning water, like everything that travels in a circle, has centripetal force. This inward force makes a space at the top of the bottle, which is filled by a rush of air that's pulled up from the bottle below. It's a mini tornado!

CRUSHING CANS

In this experiment, you'll find out what happens when a little hot water inside a hot aluminium can meets a lot of cold water. Be prepared for a bit of a bang!

YOUR TURN!

INSTRUCTIONS

1. Fill a bowl with ice-cold water. Add a few ice cubes to keep it chilly.

2. Pour water into the can so it covers the bottom but is no more than 1cm high. Too much water will produce a less dramatic result.

3. Ask an adult to heat the can over a cooker hob. When the water is boiling, you'll see a stream of steam rising from the can. The next bit has to be done quickly! Get your grown-up to grab the can with the tongs and turn it upside down, into the ice water.

4. The split-second the can hits the water, it collapses. Don't blink or you'll miss it!

WARNING: Wear goggles and have an adult supervise!

1

2

Only cover the very bottom of the can.

3

WARNING: This is where you need an adult!

WHAT'S GOING ON?

When water in the can boils, it expands and turns to steam, which fills the can. In the icy water, the steam turns back to water. The water takes up much less space than the steam did, but because the can's opening is under water, no air can rush in to take up the space. This means that there is more air pressure outside the can than inside. The outside air pushes the walls of the can inwards, and the can collapses!

4

43

BUILD A MARBLE RUN

Building a marble run is a great way to see physics in action – and also challenge your friends to a run-off! You don't need much, just some time and a few items from the recycling box. Oh, and gravity of course – but don't worry, it's always there!

YOUR TURN!

YOU WILL NEED
- A large cardboard box
- Scissors
- Sticky tape
- Double-sided tape
- Sticky tack
- Marbles
- Anything else you can find – see below

MAKING THE OBSTACLES

You can build tunnels, towers and chutes with almost anything. Have a rummage through the recycling box and see what inspires you. Here are some things that might be useful: remember to wash everything thoroughly before you start building!

- Cardboard tubes from toilet roll, cling film, kitchen paper or tin foil.
- Paper to roll into tubes
- Pipe lagging (foam insulation tubing)
- Small cardboard boxes and cartons
- Plastic drinks bottles
- Egg cartons
- Lolly sticks

MAKING A MARBLE RUN

You can build your marble run however you like – here are some tips to get you started.

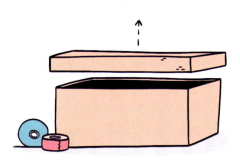

1. Choose the largest cardboard box you can find for the casing of your marble run. You can use the lid or flaps to make some fun features.

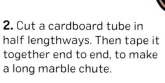

2. Cut a cardboard tube in half lengthways. Then tape it together end to end, to make a long marble chute.

3. Rolled up sheets of paper or newspaper make excellent tunnels.

4. Use scissors to cut the top and bottom off a plastic bottle. The top part can make a funnel, the middle a tunnel, and the bottom a tray to collect marbles.

5. Try out different ways of putting the elements together to make the best course for your marbles. When you're happy with your design, you can cut holes for your chutes and tunnels, then use tape or sticky tack to keep the elements in place.

Start the run high, to make the downward course as long as possible.

Make sure there are no gravity-defying upward slopes.

Tilt the shelves slightly inwards, so that the marbles don't tumble out over the edge!

This funnel is made from the top third of a plastic bottle.

The tube from a roll of cling film makes a sturdy vertical tunnel.

GLOSSARY

Astronomer
Someone who studies the Sun, Moon, planets, stars and galaxies, or everything in the Universe beyond Earth.

Atmosphere
The layer of gases surrounding Earth, held in place by gravity.

Atom
The smallest component of matter. Atoms can be combined to form molecules.

Bacteria
Microscopic, single-celled living things. Some kinds are found in rotting food; some kinds cause disease.

Bluetooth
A way of sending and receiving data over short distances using shortwave radio waves.

Centripetal
Moving towards the centre.

Condensation
The process by which a gas cools down and turns into a liquid.

Current
The flow of electricity from place to place.

Electron
A tiny particle, smaller than an atom. It is very energetic and spins fast around the centre of the atom. Electricity is produced as electrons flow from atom to atom.

Evaporation
The process by which a liquid heats up and turns into a gas.

Fluorescent
Giving off a particular kind of light. Fluorescent substances absorb one kind of radiation, such as UV light, and give off another, such as visible light.

Gravity
The force pulling objects towards each other or down to the ground.

Inertia
The tendency of an object that is not moving to stay that way and not to move.

Mass
The amount of matter – or stuff – something is made of.

Matter
Stuff. Anything that takes up space.

Medium
Something that waves can travel through. Sound waves may travel through the medium of air, water or a solid.

Molecule
The smallest possible unit of a chemical.

Orbit
To travel around something, pulled by gravity. A planet orbits a star and electrons orbit the nucleus of an atom. The path an object takes as it travels round is also called its orbit.

Particles
Small units of matter. Atoms, molecules and electrons are examples of particles.

Photon
A tiny sub-atomic (smaller than an atom) bundle of energy that we see as light.

Torpedo
A kind of underwater weapon used for blowing up ships.

Tremor
The shaking of the Earth during an earthquake.

Vacuum
Completely empty space. A vacuum contains no matter – no air, no particles at all.

Universe
Everything that exists – all of space and everything in it.

The Publisher would like to thank the following for permission to reproduce their material.

Top = t; Bottom = b; Centre = c; Left = l; Right = r

27cr kevinruss/iStock Images, 27cl, 27tc peopleimages/iStock Images, 27c ridofranz/iStock Images, 27tr orientfootage/iStock Images; 37tr CERN/Science Photo Library; 39br room the agency/Alamy Stock Photo, 39t NASA Photo/Alamy Stock Photo, 39cl alex-mit/iStock Images; 42br koto_feja/iStock Images

INDEX

THE AUTHOR & ILLUSTRATOR

DR. SHINI SOMARA

Shini's background is in mechanical engineering and fluid dynamics, but she now works as a presenter, podcaster and writer, aiming to make science and technology available to everyone. Shini has reported on climate change, food, health, energy and the physics of dark matter. She feels most comfortable when she's in the middle of an experiment or interacting with technology.

LUNA VALENTINE

Luna Valentine is a Polish children's book illustrator living in Sheffield, UK. She's inspired by science, nature and magic, and loves creating fun, lively characters who often get up to no good in their respective stories. When Luna's not drawing it's only because one of her three pet rabbits has run off with her pencil.